# Anabap

## Radical Christianity

✠

Andrew Francis

Foreword by

Jeremy Thomson

ANTIOCH PAPERS
Bristol 2010

Frst published in 2010 by
Antioch Papers, an imprint of:
Imagier Publishing
Rookery Farm
Bristol, BS35 3SY
United Kingdom
E-mail: ip@imagier.com
www.imagier.com

ISBN 13: 978-0-9558415-3-8


Cover and text design by Allan Armstrong
Cover logo designed by Priscilla Trenchard, used with
permission of the London Mennonite Centre Trustees.


Printed and bound in Great Britain by
CPI Antony Rowe, Chippenham and Eastbourne

# Table of Contents

# Foreword

Where to begin? Action or thought – or thoughtful action? We need a place to stand, somewhere to start from – it would be arrogant to imagine that we could start from scratch, make it up for ourselves.

Yet many people *are* making it up for themselves today. They are disillusioned with conventional Christianity: its toleration of injustice, its alliance with power and violence, its shallow spirituality, its bigotry, its tendency towards division. Christianity, at least as represented by the majority of churches, has disappointed, angered or rejected them, though Jesus might still be someone to believe in. The problem is that following Jesus cannot consist of an individualised spirituality; it is essentially embodied in communal life. This is because Jesus' career was oriented towards God's strategy of world-healing through calling a community to model how to live interdependently, how to value and celebrate difference, whilst constructively handling the conflicts that inevitably arise in the process.

Andrew Francis has discovered a place to stand in a movement known as Anabaptism, a tradition of Christian discipleship that goes back nearly five hundred years, though its earliest exponents traced their inspiration even further back to Jesus. It is a tradition that emphasises following Jesus, nurturing community, peace-making, and costly service. As with any tradition, it contains mistakes and follies, and yet it also imparts glimpses of genuine discipleship that can inspire and challenge contemporary believers. Anabaptism is a living tradition in the UK, embodied in a network of churches, organizations and people who seek to follow Jesus in radical ways.

In recent months Andrew Francis and I have been sharing with several other trustees in responsibility for The London Mennonite Trust, so I know that he is a thoughtful activist; he lives out what he studies and talks about. In this well-researched book he introduces the historical roots and some contemporary UK expressions of Anabaptism. If you are looking for a window with an accessible view on radical discipleship, this book is it.

Rev Dr Jeremy Thomson
London 2010

# Introduction

Imagine a radical, egalitarian, earth-friendly people's movement committed to new patterns of community, economic sharing and peace-making. Sounds too idealistic? No, because it exists both historically and in several different expressions now – each of which provides a challenge to 21$^{st}$ century living. This movement is Anabaptism – just one of several coherent and contemporary expressions of radical Christianity. Perhaps one of most popularly known Anabaptist groups today is that of the Amish – renowned for their quilts, hard work, productive farms and horse-drawn buggies (although their male hierarchy makes them possibly the least egalitarian part of the movement).

Equally important is the work of other Anabaptists, some known as Mennonites who throughout the world are involved in aid programmes and active peace-making initiatives. They are also committed to local community development work at neighbourhood level, as well as reducing their planetary carbon footprints. Involved in activist congregations, they are part of dynamic missionary growth across the world. The Amish and the Mennonites are just two of the vibrant Anabaptist groupings in today's world. What is less well known is their influence in the UK today.

Some are tempted to dismiss the Anabaptist witness simply because it is Christian. It is similar prejudice which dismisses the work of Sufis, with their inherently practical mysticism, precisely because they are Muslim *or* that ignores the power of Gandhian economics because it is rooted in an increasingly necessary decentralist and communitarian world-view *or* the plea of some aid agencies (e.g. *Christian Aid, CAFOD*, etc.) just because they are Christian. Was it not

Gandhi who said '*Blind prejudice just makes people blind to see good and will never change the world*'?

In the next few pages, you will discover that Anabaptists sought to change the world they knew, many paying with their lives. Their very name was a term of abuse yet now to the thinking enquirer it only brings questions; possibly the very reason that you are reading this. Anabaptism brings four key principles to the party:

- Vision
- Spirituality
- Community
- Practical action

Naturally, all faith groups will argue that they share these four key principles. Or at least many of the Muslim imams, Christian clergy, Buddhist teachers, Jewish rabbis and pagan leaders of my acquaintance would. But the consequent question for us all is how these are made distinctive in the faith theology and practice of the movement involved; within Anabaptism, each of these principles is distinctive.

Within the western Christian spectrum, Anabaptism sits alongside both the Salvation Army and the Quakers which invite everyone of their members to have an active commitment, every day of their lives, to the distinctive outworking of each of these four principles, in their respective movements. Again, I know many Anglican vicars, Catholic priests and Free Church ministers who, despite their public preaching, privately lament the number of those, within 'their' congregation who sit light to at least one of these principles.

Because Anabaptist-Christians do not let the Church get in the way of the teachings and life-example of Jesus, they have been mistrusted, and often persecuted, by mainstream Christians – both Protestant and Catholic. Even to this day, Anabaptists are the only Christian movement both named and condemned in the governing Thirty Nine Articles of the Church of England; as one postgraduate philosophy researcher recently told me: '*this very fact makes them worthy of serious study*'.

This short booklet aims to examine the challenge which Anabaptism can bring to life now – and for the future. In the preceding Foreword, Jeremy Thomson has also offered reasons why we can, need and should take this Christian expression to both heart and daily action; this is what is traditionally known as discipleship You can choose whether to simply read the Anabaptist challenge in the narrative which follows or pursue its detail through the footnotes and references, enabling further study.

Whilst there are many and detailed Anabaptist histories available, the next chapter seeks to highlight the various roots of the movement – the social circumstances of each challenged, then helped define the movement's emphases. These 'core practices' are explained in a short six-part subsequent chapter. The penultimate chapter examines the nature of the four key principles (shown above), briefly exploring their practical implications for discipleship today. The final chapter surveys the current Anabaptist scene from a UK perspective, revealing both a breadth of growing influence and active issues which Anabaptists could help wider society engage with. Finally, some thumbnail biographies of UK Anabaptists, an annotated booklist and a web directory offer you the opportunity to explore '*The Anabaptist Challenge*' more fully. Let me invite you on a journey into the heart of the Anabaptist witness.

# Roots

Peter Weir's 1985 film *Witness, starring Harrison Ford, is aptly named.* It tells how a Philadelphia detective has to hide Amish witnesses to a big-city murder back in their own agrarian community. The detective both struggles with and learns to appreciate the rich traditions of the particular Amish yet Anabaptist heritage. It is indeed a witness to a counter-culture whose life-affirming values embrace so much of that which is *not* of the detective's own lifestyle and world-view.

This centrality of 'witness' is key to understanding nearly all of Anabaptism – as it will be for almost every expression of radical Christianity. The lives of Anabaptist Christians, both historically and today, are deliberately forged to be a witness to those around them. Just as the word 'Christian' was coined pejoratively at Antioch to describe followers of Jesus, so the word 'Anabaptist' was derisively used by the persecuting witnesses of these later radical Christians.

Like all strong, growing plants, the Anabaptist movement has a multiplicity of roots. At least three geographic areas of simultaneous, fertile beginning can be identified. Each of these brought distinctive witness to the movement as these groups interacted, then cohered into a vibrant stream of Christianity.

## Fertile Ground

Late medieval western Europe was a patchwork of small kingdoms, some of which sufficiently co-operated together to forge themselves as identifiable nations/countries. Yet all were part of what has since become known as Christendom – the area presided over by the Roman Catholic Church, led by the Pope. There was no option: to be a citizen meant being a part of the

Church of Rome. Orthodoxy was demanded and dissent was punishable by excommunication, exile and sometimes death.

The power of such a trans-national Church was all-pervasive, subjugating not just individuals, be they peasant, priest or feudal lord, but often nations as well. The Church had huge wealth, demanding tithes and owning vast tracts of land. Reaction became inevitable – both socially and spiritually – from priests, people, scholars and theologians.

One such reaction was that of a Roman Catholic monk, Martin Luther, whose reading of the Bible led him to publish 95 Theses, or propositions for change, in October 1517. He translated the Bible into German, wrote vernacular hymns, and called for reform of the Church. More personally, rejecting celibacy, he married and was only protected from the Vatican's fury by the local prince in whose fiefdom he lived.

Also in that same early sixteenth century, a series of bloody local skirmishes since denominated as the German Peasants War, occurred. Many of these local uprisings were led by priests, who were far more committed to their people and parishes than to the Pope. To survive, some practised a basic 'community of goods', sharing food, clothing, shelter and other resources; this practice simply followed the biblical example of the early Christian Church (recorded in Acts 2 and 4) but demonstrated how biblical practice was life-giving against the crushing rents, taxes and tithes of a monolithic Church.[1] This religiously inspired peasant movement became known as the *Bundschuh* [Ger. people's shoe] Movement after the common

---

[1] cf. *The German Peasants War and Anabaptists Community of Goods*, James Stayer, London, McGill Queens UP, 1991.

working boots worn by nearly everyone except the aristocracy and senior clergy.

## Zurich

Amongst those influenced by Luther's theological stance, the social unrest and the contemporary egalitarian humanism of Erasmus was Ulrich Zwingli, who had been called to be the preacher/presiding minister of the cathedral of the city-state of Zurich. Naturally, his supporting lay leaders were educated men, versed in biblical languages and able to afford their own printed Bibles. When Zwingli preached reform, his parishioners listened but his lay leaders were troubled at Zwingli's illogicality in not pushing for total reform and rejection of Catholic teaching. These lay leaders rejected the Lenten imposition of fasting by eating sausages in reaction to the ban. On one such occasion of meeting together, their biblical reading led them to baptize each other as believers. This was not just in contravention of Catholic teaching but of Zwingli's stance and Zurich's laws. The three key leaders soon died; Grebel of the plague, Mainz and Blaurock were outlawed, tried and executed.[2] Hindsight shows that it was these martyrs who were far more logical in their pattern of biblical reform, by rejecting man-made liturgical restrictions and infant baptism, than Zwingli and the Zurich authorities

For centuries, Zurich was deemed to be the birthplace of the movement of 're-baptisers' [Ger: *wiedertaufer*] or 'Ana-baptists'. But this is a false picture. At least two other major hotbeds of radical reform are known and historically

---

[2]    *Anabaptist Portraits*, John Allen Moore. Scottdale, Herald Press, 1984.

defined as Anabaptist roots in alpine southern Germany and the northern Netherlands marshland.

## SOUTHERN EUROPE

Leading 'voices' in the German Peasants War were Michael Sattler and Balthasar Hubmaier, then both Catholic priests whose reading of the Bible led them to reject the Church-and-State complicity exemplified in Zurich's attitudes. They argued for the local church to be a voluntary association of believers, made up of those baptised upon their personal confession of faith in Jesus Christ as Lord and Saviour. In 21st century Britain, this stance seems both logical and reasonable as increasing questions grow about Church–State links and the notion that baptism (implying church membership) should be administered to non-consenting children.

Both Sattler and Hubmaier are primarily associated with the Swiss Brethren. They were persecuted to execution for perpetrating such heresy in the eyes of the Christendom Church, which saw such dissent as capable of eroding its power. Before their respective deaths, Sattler had helped draft the decisive Seven Articles of the Schleitheim Confession and Hubmaeir's later published correspondence gave theological weight to the movement. The Schleitheim Confession[3] was the first widely accepted Anabapatist confession of faith, giving shape to the growing Swiss branch of the movement.

Anabaptist influence spread both by word of mouth and the writings of those like Sattler and Hubmaier. The latter's presence turned the city of Nicholsburg towards Anabaptist ideals in 1526/7 but a series (now well-known) disputations

---

[3]     Trans, John Howard Yoder, Scottdale, Herald Press, 1973.

with other early Anabaptist leaders helped forge the movement's thinking. One such leader was a travelling bookseller, Hans Hut, who gave away proselytising tracts to his customers; he too was tried and executed.[4] Against the background of such persecution, and later banishment, small groups of southern European Anabaptists fled eastwards. Naturally, they shared what little they had, drawing on lessons from the Peasants War, developing a greater sense of the 'community of goods'.

They found sanctuary on the lands of Moravian nobles, who were happy to shelter them in exchange for manual labour on the land. Leaders such as Peter Riedemann and Jakob Hutter emerged; the latter giving his name to an assembling company of Hutterites. At first they slept in barns, then built similarly large communal houses, known as *Hof* from the German; so each of the individual house communities became known as a *Bruderhof*.[5] Centuries later, a separate movement known as the *Bruderhof* arose from the Hutterite movement still with extended households, to practise more communitarian industry than agriculture.

These historical agriculturally based communities, and the later Amish, all with a commitment to hard work on the land, have helped give the movement an 'earth friendly' profile. In more recent times this profile has been reaffirmed by the wartime efforts of the English Bruderhof, then pioneering pilot

---

[4]     *Swiss Anabaptism*, John Howard Yoder, Herald Press, Scottdale, 1973.

[5]     *The Believers' Church*, Donald Durnbaugh, Scottdale, Herald Press, 1985.

agricultural projects in the Americas[6] and global Mennonite rural relief work projects. Resulting articles in UK national newspapers and specialist agricultural journals have brought this part of the movement to the attention of a wide audience, popularly altering the perception of its radical Christian trajectory to one of 'back-to-the-land' movement

### NORTHERN NETHERLANDS

North-western Europe is a long way from Rome and the tentacles of its papal envoys. Thinkers like Erasmus encouraged a logical response to everything – including reading the Bible. Priests troubled by Catholic excesses became persuaded of ideas such as 'community of goods' and believers' baptism, gradually encouraging their parishioners towards these ideals. They were becoming Anabaptist by default in following the patterns which the Jesus of the Gospels exemplified. After a series of theological and leadership struggles, one itinerant leader emerged in the north Netherlands region of Friesland, named Menno Simons, whose persecuted congregations became known as Mennonites.[7] Already Anabaptism began to have defining emphases and known groups; within a generation, an Amsterdam Mennonite baker sheltered dissident English Christians who returned to found the English Baptist movement.

Tragically, Anabaptism suffered a lasting stain when a small, isolated group of aberrant leaders brought the movement

[6] *Earthkeepers,* Art & Jocele Meyer, Scottdale, Herald Press, 1991.

[7] *Dutch Anabaptism*, Cornelius Krahn, The Hague, Martin Nijhoff, 1968.

into justified disrepute. This was at Munster (in nearby Germany), where a few misguided Anabaptists tried to set up an Anabaptist city, forcibly demanding 'community of goods' and polygamy, with disastrous results for all. Thousands actually tried to join them but were turned back by the authorities.[8]

The regional Catholic authorities brought a violent end to this, having first besieged the city. The three leaders were executed horribly and their grisly remains left on display in cages hung high on the castle walls. Walking around Munster Zoo today, one looks up to see facsimile cages still hanging on the castle walls, as a reminder of this tragedy. Unfortunately, this singular aberrant example has disproportionally tarred the whole ongoing movement.

### A GROWING MOVEMENT

Meanwhile, in eastern Europe the group known as the Czech Brethren were gaining a higher profile for their re-baptising views, their separatist stance with regard to Church and State and their pacifist commitment. They found a voice in their most influential leader, Peter Chelcisky. These Brethren had evolved from the excesses of the earlier Taborite and Adamite groups and used Chelcisky's wise leadership to articulate their now pacifist separatism, thus distancing them from their messy roots.

In 1556, they even invited Calvin and other reformers to meet with them in Poland to debate the true outworking of

8   *Narrative of the Anabaptist Madness: The Overthrow of Munster, the Famous Metropolis of Westphalia* (Studies in the History of Christian Thought) (Vols. 1 & 2), H. Von Kerssenbrock & C. S. Mackay, London, Brill, 2007.

Reformed faith and discipleship.[9] As more of the Czech Brethren's writings are discovered and translated, there is a growing academic argument to consider the Czech Brethren as yet another Anabaptist root but not all scholars are yet convinced of this. Further west, Anabaptists fled to Elizabethan England, but even there they were not safe. In 1575, two Anabaptists were sentenced for exhorting their beliefs and horribly burned at the stake at Smithfield in London. A third Anabaptist, despite similar sentence, managed to escape. Anabaptists continue to be deemed a subversive threat to the Church of England so that they were the only dissenting group to be condemned within the defining Anglican Thirty Nine Articles, which remains unchanged in the 21st century.

Despite this, the majority of Dutch migrants were Anabaptists and by 1587 these migrants constituted the majority of Norwich's population.[10] Extant historical records from this era point to the presence of Anabaptists in other East Anglian towns, Lincolnshire and the south-east midlands as well as London. However, the slur of Munster and ongoing persecution meant that most English Anabaptists went 'underground' joining Brownist congregations. The latter were part of an English Separatist movement, rejecting the Church–State connection whilst affirming believing-adult profession of faith. There is sufficient academic speculation to

---

[9] *Communalism*, Kenneth Rexroth, New York, Seabury Press, 1974.

[10] *The Radical Reformation (third edition), p. 1205, George Huntston Williams, Kirksville, Sixteenth Century Journal Publishers, 1992.*

recognize the Anabaptist influence if not name,[11] which travelled into the later Quaker and Independent congregational movements.

During this same period, Anabaptist stirrings occurred in eastern Europe. A separatist movement known as the Polish Minor Church was riven with discussions about pacifism, community and the nature of Christ. A pacifist group calling themselves the Polish Brethren emerged. They practised some 'community of goods' across their extended households and adult profession of faith in their congregations. Their key leader was Faustus Socinus, who later renounced the need for believers' baptism, becoming personally infamous for stirring up unorthodox views about the divine and human natures of Jesus.[12]

However, despite the fact that the Polish Brethren were ultimately subsumed back into the Minor Church, there is increasing academic support for *considering* the Polish Brethren as another of Anabaptism's several roots; the word 'consider' is important because there are arguments in both directions. As well as groups that became identified as the roots of Anabptism, there were individuals whose work and teaching were catalysts for the growth of ideas and practices among those groups. One was Andreas Karlstadt who, having been one of Martin Luther's key mentors, went on to seriously delineate

[11]   *The Admonition Controversy*, Donald J. McGinn, New Brunswick, Rutgers UP, 1949.

[12]   *Luther and the False Brethgren*, Mark U. Edwards, Stanford, Stanford UP, 1975.

the *Gelassenheit* or 'yieldedness' principle,[13] we return to this later. Thomas Muntzer was another 'Peasants' War leader', who also saw such 'yieldedness' as essential, particularly in his nurture and formation of proto-Anabaptist groups which in their turn helped to practise the Anabaptist vision for community. Another influence was Caspar Schwenkfeld, whose leanings towards an individualistic mystical Spiritualism meant that his extended dialogues with Anabaptist leaders, such as Pilgram Marpeck in South Germany, helped Anabaptism define its richer practical spirituality, drawing on the Rhineland mystics and the activism of egalitarian radicals as well as the reforming logic of scripturally based communities of faith. These diverse individuals exerted considerable influence upon the nascent Anabaptist movement, demonstrating something of its fragility in its shaping by those who are sometimes seen with opposing views to the movement. Many early Anabaptists, including their leaders, had short lives, suffering torture either before execution, escape or exile. '*Anabaptist leaders tended to articulate theological positions ad hoc*'[14] then and now; there was never time to write a sy tematic theology. Instead they worked out their discipleship, in other words how they practised their faith, refining it as they ran and when they stopped to share the story of Jesus. Those core practices form the subject of our next chapter.

[13]
    *Karlstadt as the Father of Baptist Movements: the Emergence of Lay Protestantism*, p.46, Calvin Pater, Toronto: University of Toronto Press, 1984.

[14]
    *Building Communities of Compassion: Mennonite Mutual Aid in Theory and Practice*, p. 121, John D. Roth, Scottdale, Herald Press, 1998.

# Core Practices

Some years ago, I was staying in a southern European village and a circus pitched on the central square. Folk watched in alarm as both a trapeze and a high-wire were slung between two high-sided lorries either side of the ring. The later audience was relieved to see the acrobats perform above a taut net suspended between six outward-facing poles.

The practice of Anabaptist-flavoured Christian discipleship is like that net. It is held in tension between six outward-facing 'poles' of understanding and practice. These six 'poles' or core practices can be identified as a movement that is:

- Jesus–centred

- Peace–making

- Adult–faith confessing

- Church–State separating

- Community–building

- People–serving

That is quite an agenda. This short chapter seeks to look briefly at the understanding of each of these six core practices.

### JESUS–CENTRED

Anabaptist-flavoured Christianity fits in the orthodox mainstream of belief. It is Trinitarian by nature, affirming one God in three persons or expressions: the Creator God of all, Jesus as Saviour and the Spirit who empowers the life of faith. But if we are to follow the way of the Jesus, who became known as the Christ and whose followers were therefore called Christians, it is first to the life, teaching and ministry of Jesus

14

that we should look for direct understanding of who God is. This is classic Anabaptist theology.

In using Jesus as the primary way to understand the circle-of-expression that is God, we have a living human example upon which to model our human living. To do this does not deny the divinity of Jesus but merely emphasizes that we share a common humanity. Therefore, this determines the way in which Anabaptists read and value the Bible.[1]

Clearly, each of the four Gospels provides us with a portrait of Jesus. Obviously, each Gospel writer ensures that he includes those emphases and episodes of Jesus' earthly ministry which will be of most encouragement to that writer's intended audience. As with any reported account, the inclusion of particular speeches, phrases and words is the product of human memory and open to interpretation. What is vital is that there is not only much correlation in the four Gospel narratives of Jesus' life but consistency in the nature of Jesus' teaching, pronouncements and attitudes to all. Therefore, given such a coherent example of Jesus' life and words, it behoves those who claim to be his followers to adopt his attitudes and example as well as heeding his teaching directly. Thus Anabaptists have a natural suspicion of those who seek to adapt or dilute Jesus' teaching for their own and/or others' purposes. Naturally, this elicits serious questions from Anabaptists of those, including the institutional Church, whose teaching contradicts what Anabaptists perceive as Jesus' own way. This ideal of following in the path of Jesus is central to Anabaptist patterns of

[1]    *Biblical Interpretation in the Anabaptist Tradition*, Stuart Murray, Ontario, Pandora Press, 2000.

discipleship.[2] This way of 'following after', commonly called *Nachfolge* from the German, is a common term both in books and Anabaptist conversation.

This commitment to the Jesus way aligns Anabaptists much more to the pietism and asceticism of the late medieval mystical tradition than to the scriptural focus of classic Protestantism. Living out Jesus' example, simply and prayerfully, is far more important to Anabaptists than whether you have read so many chapters of scripture each day. So much so that Anabaptism has often been described as 'neither Protestant nor Catholic'.[3]

Whilst personal faith had to be an unforced, mature decision to follow the way of Jesus, Anabaptists recognized their need to live alongside and travel with their fellow believers for mutual encouragement. This shared journey also emulated the pattern of Jesus and his disciples. Thus the Anabaptist's personal decision echoed the individualism of Protestantism whilst the role of the 'believing community' echoed the ecclesial emphasis of more catholic traditions.

Affirming 'Jesus is Lord' and modelling one's life upon his does not protect the disciple from suffering, as many Anabaptists discovered. It does recognise and acknowledge the orthodoxy (right belief) of Anabaptism, as well as the movement's inherent orthopraxy (right practical attitudes), which gave both the movement and its adherents a visibility,

---

[2]     *Following in the Footsteps of Christ*, Arnold Snyder, London, Darton, Longman & Todd, 2004.

[3]     *Anabaptism: Neither Protestant nor Catholic,* Walter Klaassen, New York, Conrad Press, 1973.

leaving them open to persecution by those who accepted a different understanding of holistic faith and discipleship.

### PEACE–MAKING

Historic Anabaptism quickly adopted a peace-making tradition, which came straight from the teaching of Jesus. Contemporary Anabaptism is marked by a wide-ranging commitment to peace-making.

As already discovered, itinerant 16th century Anabaptists could not always rely on safety of numbers. They were persecuted unto death by both Catholic and Protestant authorities so to travel in large groups easily attracted attention. To travel alone made them prey for thieves, vagabonds and even the wolves and bears – all common across middle Europe then. Therefore, it is no surprise that early Anabaptist groups and leaders debated whether you should be a sword-bearer [*Die Schwertler*] or a staff-bearer [*Die Stabler*]. The defining 1527 *Schleitheim Confession* of the early Swiss Anabaptists forbade the use of the sword, and logically all weapons capable of lethal force. What was agreed by some took longer to become the accepted position of all[4], yet the renunciation of weapons quickly occurred.

There were some with influence across the early movement like Hubmaier,[5] who supported the restricted use of force, including both the sword and lethally so by magistrates

---

4    *Anabaptists and the Sword*, James Stayer, New York, Wipf & Stock, 2002.

5    *Balthasar Hubmaier: Theologian of Anabaptism,* Ed, H. Wayne Pipkin & John Howard Yoder, Scottdale, Mennonite Publishing Network, 1989.

or within just wars. In parts, this position survived into second generation Anabaptism, such as among the Batenburgers of the Netherlands. Such views were opposed then by pacifist Anabaptists, and continue to be so; one of the several reasons for this was the horror and recoil of the whole movement to the tragedy which occurred at Munster.

Munster's aberration and general societal violence still drive Anabaptists, in every generation, to re-examine Jesus' teaching to '*turn the other cheek*' and to forgive those who persecute you. The logic runs that if Jesus asks us not to strike back and recognize that we should forgive our persecutors, we will encounter violence but we should not retaliate. As the generations go by and Anabaptists have experienced different forms of oppression and persecution, the answer has consistently been to adopt a position of non-violence.[6] What is also consistently and profoundly recognized is that Anabaptists are called to be active peace-makers and reconcilers.

Jesus teaching in Matthew 18 vv.15–18 is a model for all Christians, not just Anabaptists who instill this in themselves and their children as the way to live. It teaches that if you have a difficulty or problem, you should go to the perpetrator seeking resolution and only then gradually escalate the options. Within the last decade, many have displayed the Mennonite Central Committee's poster, with this John Stoner quote: "A modest proposal for peace: let the Christians of the world agree they will not kill each other." If the Mennonites who had followed this teaching over the centuries had been heeded in their calls

---

[6]  E.g. *He is Our Peace: Meditations on Christian Nonviolence,* Ed., Emmy Barth, Robertsbridge, Plough Publishing House, 1994.

for peace all would be living in a safer and more unified world today.

It has been that Mennonite sub-set of Anabaptism that has been most active in developing 'peace theology'[7] and in challenging the prevailing military culture.[8] Sometimes this work has been done at very practical levels alongside Quaker activists and scholars. Yet the ongoing contemporary non-violent, peace-making examples of the Mennonites' Anabaptist cousins, the Amish[9] and Bruderhof/Hutterian communities[10] tell of a whole movement that is recognized for its peace stance. This establishes the movement as one of the 'historic peace-churches'.

At a more localized level, this has also involved practical Mennonite commitment to conflict mediation programmes. The work of Chicago's Lombard Institute has gained a worldwide reputation in this field. It was their team that inspired and enabled the staff and work of *Bridge Builders*, a conflict mediation service set up by and at the London Mennonite Centre (more of this in the next chapter). Over the last generation, north American Mennonite groups have funded neighbourhood workers in Ireland to help foster better Protestant–Catholic inter-relations.

---

[7] *Essays on Peace Theology and Witness,* Ed., William M. Swartley, Elkhart, Institute of Mennonite Studies, 1988.

[8] *When War is Unjust,* John Howard Yoder, Maryknoll NY, Orbis, 1996.

[9] *Amish and the State,* Ed., Donald B. Kraybill, Baltimore, John S. Hopkins University, 1993.

[10] *Seeking Peace,* Johann Christoph Arnold, Robertsbridge, Plough Publishing House, 1998.

In north America, Europe and the UK, various Anabaptist partners are active participants in the creation of Victim and Offender Reconciliation Programmes, further extending the peace-making tradition in this reconciliation process. Other individuals are active in the often trans-global campaigns to support political prisoners and to abolish capital punishment.

### ADULT–FAITH CONFESSING

There is sufficient documentary evidence that one of the earliest gatherings of (those later identified as) the Swiss Brethren involved a clear call to profess their active faith as adult believers.[11] This resulted in all the believers gathered in Felix Manz's Zurich home being baptised as professing adults; the story was briefly shared in the previous chapter.

Elsewhere, those like Andreas Karlstadt, Thomas Muntzer and Caspar Schwenkfeld were formative influences upon the nascent movement. Snyder, the Canadian Anabaptist notes "*Although neither Karlstadt, Muntzer or Schwenkfeld took the step of re-baptising adults on confession of faith, nevertheless they provided the essential logic for the practice of adult baptism by their critique of the practice of infant baptism.*"[12] Elsewhere those more indentifiable as Anabaptist leaders, as far apart as southern Germany and the northern Netherlands, all came to the conviction and practice, from reading the Bible, that adult profession of faith was necessary.

---

[11] *Glimpses of Mennonite History and Doctrine,* pp.24-5, John C. Wenger, Scottdale, Herald Press, 1947.

[12] *Anabaptist History and Theology,* p.46, C. Arnold Snyder, Ontario, Pandora Press, 1995.

For Anabaptists scripture was and is uncompromising – this meant baptism as confessing believers.

Believers' baptism became a defining mark of this new movement. Less than a decade before they had predominantly been a group of religiously inspired peasants, disgruntled by their earthly lot, but galvanized and led by independently minded priests, like Muntzer. They saw their struggle as one of faith against a monolithic Church, which worked with the vested interests of the state and economic power, to suppress their own life and faith.[13] Catching the vision of Jesus' egalitarian kingdom, meant standing up to be counted and joining the dissenting radicals. The Peasants War had a broader 'reach' than early Anabaptism as only a much smaller proportion of these dissenters went on to be baptised as believers, thus identifiable as Anabaptists; but the connections are historically verifiable.

Denigration and persecution of the movement went together. As already explained they were called *Wiedertaufer* or re-baptisers. This term, translated as 'Anabaptist' was used just as centuries before persecutors at Antioch had used the term 'Christian' in the same way [Acts 11 v. 26]. Again the name stuck and a movement was born.

What was vital to this new expression of discipleship was not so much the act of baptism as a believer, but the confession of mature personal faith. This was in response to the free grace of God, revealed through the life, death and resurrection of Jesus Christ. Persecution and other circumstances often meant that such baptisms were performed

[13]    *Faith in the Revolution,* Andrew Bradstock, London: SPCK, 1997.

by sprinkling or pouring water from a jug. The common, and biblically derived, image of being immersed in a river or pond whilst ideal could only happen in more rural and/or less threatening situations.[14]

Just as in Paul's New Testament writings, baptism is referred to as dying and rising with Christ. It is the yielding to God's greater purposes – possibly unto death – that is important. Some of the earliest Anabaptist martyrs were executed by drowning as the State's warning to those who wished to repudiate State-sanctioned infant baptism. Paul's teaching should have been words of comfort to these drowning martyrs. This 'yieldedness' is an important part of Anabaptism. Just as individuals yield to the way of Christ in making their own personal testimony, so they also accept that they yield to the corporate pattern of the group of individuals with whom they share the faith journey. This 'yieldedness' (as initially explained in the previous chapter) is known as *Gelassenheit* – which like *Nachfolge* (see above) is a term often seen in books or heard in Anabaptist conversations.

Nearly every Christian movement will declare that a definable moment of personal profession of faith is vital for the ongoing nurture of discipleship. What makes Anabaptism different is its rejection of any rite imposed by Church, parents or State on a non-professing child or infant, however strong parental faith is, which claims to have either the divine efficacy or role that a later/adult rite of profession has.

---

[14]     *Believers' Baptism*, Marlin Jeshke, Scottdale, Herald Press, 1985.

## CHURCH–STATE SEPARATING

However, if you were a 're-baptiser', this meant that you were deemed to have already been baptised. Infant baptism was normally a State-sanctioned Church rite. To be baptized again, in the eyes of Church and State, meant the rejection of the validity of what they had already sanctioned. This marked you as dissenting not just from the Church's teaching and practice but as rejecting the State's right to determine how faith should be ordered.

It is hardly surprising therefore that the Anabaptist movement incurred the wrath and consequent persecution by the Church authorities, both Catholic and Protestant. To have accepted such dissent would have threatened the complicit relationship between the Church and the State. To protect that relationship's balance, such dissenters have to be deemed as heretics, therefore inviting the full sanction of the law, namely persecution and exile or execution. Biblical scholars see a similar complicity and conspiracy between the Jewish religious leaders and the then occupying Roman authorities in the trial and execution of Jesus.[15]

The prevailing Church-State relationship is what became western Christendom, which in every century has adopted patterns of persecution of those who dissented. Historically, Anabaptists gathered together the stories of their martyrs' extraordinary courage as they faced the executioner's

[15] *The Politics of Jesus,* John Howard Yoder, Scottdale, Herald Press, 1994.

axe, drowning weights or the stake. Standard academic texts make reference to these works.[16]

As previously noted, the Church of England's official stance is condemnatory of Anabaptism. Again it is not surprising that many contemporary Anabaptists seek to engage in constructive dialogue to remove this slur, whilst maintaining a healthy critique of those patterns of Establishment which continue to uphold a Church–State complicity.[17] Modern Anabaptism calls for this to change; without the State's protection, perhaps all Christians could recover their missionary calling, offering a truer witness without the Churches trappings of wealth and power? We return to this subject in the final chapter.

## COMMUNITY-BUILDING

In their reading of the Bible, Anabaptists have come to perceive community as operating at three levels: globally, at neighbourhood level and as 'communities of believers'. Some of the logic for this has been rehearsed in the previous chapter.

Anabaptists acknowledge Jesus as the Lord and Head of all creation as the New Testament Letter to the Colossians states [chap 1 v.26]. This means that they see the world's population as a global community who are sustained by their life on earth together. This has a two-fold outworking. Firstly, it means taking Jesus' example seriously to treat every other human being as though they are our brother or our sister; therefore we

---

16  *Anabaptist History and Theology,* C. Arnold Snyder, Ontario Pandora Press, 1995.

17  *Church and State – Uneasy Alliances,* Stewart Lamont, London, The Bodley Head, 1989.

must do nothing which harms their welfare, such as going to war against them or living unsustainably on the planet. This latter is the second outworking in that we have to live more responsibly and accountably towards one another for the sake of all on God's earth.

Historically, the original Anabaptist communities were shortlived. Having briefly explored how in the intervening centuries, different Anabaptist streams such as the communitarian Bruderhof and the agrarian Amish have emerged, it is the contemporary relevance of the Anabaptist need to build community to which we now turn our attention. The next chapter includes some practical exploration of what this 'community-building' means within the Anabaptist world-view. Just as within an understanding of global peace-making, Anabaptism does not encourage nationalism, which in turn leads to division between peoples. Many of my Stateside friends are distinctly uneasy in the daily honouring of the Stars and Stripes and the hand-on-heart singing of the *Star Spangled Banner*. For them this has dreadful echoes of Romans, both soldiers and citizens, paying homage to the Emperor. In today's world is *Pax Americana* the new *Pax Romana*?

Following the way of Jesus makes us citizens of his kingdom first, citizens of his world next and only then do we have any kind of national identity; to put loyalty to country first is to invert God's purpose for his people.[18] To talk of God's economy for the world, or the household of God, becomes impossible if it is attempted from a position of sectarian

[18]   *For the Nations,* John Howard Yoder, Cambridge, Eerdmans, 1997.

nationalism; an example would be those declaring *"For Queen and Country"* as their primary maxim.

The nature of the egalitarian, consensual, Anabaptist politic, partially rooted in a peasants' movement to overturn injustices, seemingly makes it leftward leaning.[19] However, the movement's anti-totalitarianism makes it much more of a democratic, decentralist community, favouring federalism between countries and congregations. This naturally aligns it with much green ideology in its stance towards the planet and in building up neighbourhood structures which nurture local community. It is rare to find an Anabaptist who is not involved in some non-church-based neighbourhood or community activity.

That federalism spills over into shared Christian life. Congregations perceive themselves as 'communities of believers'. Each congregation chooses to align itself with others around particular confessional statements to which all can assent. Historically this began with the Swiss Brethren's 1527 *Schleitheim Confession* and continues today.[20] Such alliances are relational rather than hierarchical, with any shared appointments being of service and/or secretarial functions. When referred to as 'a denomination', friends in the Mennonite Church of the USA smile politely, but often shudder within as they realize their shared identity causes others to make wrong assumptions. Yet other Anabaptist denominations, and their members, are more centrist. In 2009 in the UK, following

[19] *God's Left Wing,* Alan Kreider, London, LMC, 1985.

[20] *One Lord, One Church, One Hope and One God: Mennonite Confessions of Faith*, Ed. Howard J. Loewen, Elkhart, Institute of Mennonite Studies, 1985.

requested consultations, the Anabaptist Network began a 'Network of congregations/communities', deliberately employing such terms to imply the nature of the relationship.

Within such congregations, their shared life and worship is to demonstrate a Jesus ethic of "welcome and bread for all". Increasingly UK Anabaptists are turning the accepted academic perception of Christianity as behaving-believing-belonging,[21] recognizing that welcome, inclusion and belonging may be the best seed-bed in which to nurture life-long discipleship. The present but fragile success of the Anabaptist-oriented *Urban Expression* church-planting teams in cities across Britain and their related *Crucible* training course is a further demonstration that 'community-building' in Jesus' ways is contemporarily possible; how much lasting effect they can have will depend upon the willingness of others to utilise their methodology.[22]

### PEOPLE–SERVING

The next chapter's fourth defining principle, 'Practical Action', serves as a further effective introduction to this focus of 'people-serving'. Jesus' injunction about himself, *'The Son of Man came not be served but to serve'*, is the decisive personal model for all Anabaptists. Jesus also reminds us that whether it is feeding the hungry, clothing the naked, housing the homeless, although this is done for others we are doing it for him [Matt. 25 vv. 31–46]. Such teachings are a manifesto for service. Jesus' instruction to *'Seek first the kingdom'* is not an

---

21    *Religion in Britain Since 1945,* Grace Davies ,Oxford Blackwells,1994.

22    *Church Planting in the inner City: the Urban Expression Story,* Juliet Kilpin, Nottingham, Grove Books, 2007.

inward, mystical journey only but a call to look prayerfully at the needs of his world and our neighbourhoods afresh.

Living out the Sermon on the Mount of Matthew chapters 5–7 creates a lifetime's agenda.[23] I recall Simon Mayo, the BBC radio presenter, saying that he would personally prefer to be called a 'Mountie' because of Jesus' teaching (predominantly that in the 'Sermon on the Mount'), rather than a Christian with all the horror that implies historically, given its Christendom connotations full of Crusades and other religious wars.

The apostle Paul reminds us that *'there are varieties of service but the same Lord'*. Nowhere is this more true than in the global network of Anabaptist expressions. Internationally, the Amish are known for their county-wide team work in 'barn raising' together as well as financially supporting one another in times of need. The UK's Bruderhof communities are renowned for their high quality, relatively inexpensive wooden play equipment, designed for the handicapped and pre-schoolers; many groups and parents testify to this. Elsewhere, reference has been made to the work of Mennonite agencies in the face of global emergency; as I write Mennonite acquaintances are working in Haitian relief programmes following the earthquake there. Again, reference has been made to Anabaptist-rooted 'conflict mediation' agencies across the world; these are also involved in training others to set up further similar agencies.

Naturally, my Roman Catholic friends will point towards *Caritas*, the global relief partnership which the UK's CAFOD, 'their' aid agency, is involved with or the

---

[23]   *Kingdom Citizens*, John Driver, Scottdale, Herald Press, 1980.

neighbourhood action and care which local Catholic Worker groups have instilled. The same is true for friends across many denominations. All can talk of individuals who do this or that. But they will be hard pressed to talk of complete local congregations where everyone is automatically expected to be involved in some particular form of serving people directly. I recall the unresolved difficulties that every United Reformed Church member *should have to* join the boycotts of, at the time, South African then later Nestle products, because of apartheid and the 'baby-milk scandals' respectively.

This shared commitment is not just the Anabaptist distinctive, it is the expectation of belonging to this 'community of faith'. One French Mennonite told me *'Anabaptists do service like Moslems do five-fold prayers every day; it is the pattern of our lives, it's our way of following Jesus'*. Equally, one Mennonite pastor of my acquaintance grumbles about how difficult it is to persuade his congregation that this should be their norm. Despite their ideals, Mennonites are very human in their everyday pressures.

This chapter turns full circle as the touchstone for 'serving people' returns to that wandering Hebrew teacher called Jesus, who spoke consistently of the kingdom of God, healed the sick in body, mind and spirit, ate with his friends and prayed quietly alone. Parsing up the narratives of the Gospels' writers, this four-fold emphasis, of teaching/preaching, healing, socialising and praying, emerges in almost equal measures. This is the Jesus blueprint for his kingdom's people. It is more action than talk in a cycle of action, contemplation and reflection.

When Jesus told the narrative of the Good Samaritan – the foreigner who cared for his enemy – he invited his listeners to consider *"Who is my neighbour?"*. Hearing that parable again now, it is not possible to limit our caricatured answers to the unemployed man or depressed new mum down our street, or the kids with time on their hands in the local park. In 2010, our neighbours cry out from Haiti just as they did from South East Asia in the wake of the Boxing Day tsunami. As individuals, we may struggle to see how we can serve them but there are ways if we are part of globally thinking 'communities of compassion' who choose and know how to act locally. Anabaptism's Jesus-shaped vision attempts that.

# Principles

There are many ways of cutting a cake. Equally, there are many ways of defining a movement. Some will argue that it should be on the basis of the movement's own 'core practices'. Others will argue that principles should be defined first, then patterns of behaviour, that is practices, should be worked out secondarily. Such discussion may work in the philosophy classroom but not in the active theatre of Christian discipleship. Core practices and principles are symbiotic; they are both living and evolving entities, sharing in a dynamic inter-relationship, cross-fertilising to each other's mutual benefit.

As stated in the Introduction, Anabaptism has four key principles in its movement:

- Vision

- Spirituality

- Community

- Practical action

Hints of these principles could be seen in the historic roots of the movement (our first chapter) and in the core practices (our second chapter) as they developed 'on the hoof' – an appropriate image for the *Bundschuh* people's movement. Some parts of these principles were directly addressed in the movement's own declarations of faith, such as the 1527 *Schleitheim Confession* ( previously referred to).

### VISION

Each part of the contemporary Anabaptist movement is driven by a particular interpretation of the broad Anabaptist vision. We have already identified that agenda as a

Jesus-centred, peace-making, Church–State separating, adult-faith confessing, community-building, people-serving movement. That is quite a vision.

In 1944 a north American academic, Harold S. Bender, rehabilitated Anabaptism as a mainstream yet radical Reformation movement. He delineated a geographically single-sourced Anabaptist vision.[1] Alongside others, Bender had been active in promulgating outward and open relations from the Mennonite cause towards society and a breadth of denominational traditions (e.g. Presbyterian, Episcopalian, etc.) that had perceived them as sectarian. In north America, many had previously viewed Mennonites (if they knew anything about them) as 'anonymous Amish' who lived simply and quietly amidst an increasingly materialist post-war culture. Often they were known as 'the quiet in the land'.

The work of Mennonite mission agencies even caught the positive attention of the United States Government, who looked increasingly to these agencies for guidance, assistance and often leadership in various international and domestic situations of crisis. As other more established, and possibly more conservative, denominational agencies appeared to question the Mennonites' upstart status, it became apparent that it was their coherent vision of practical Christian discipleship and service which had created such credibility. Yet each instance of partnership with a secular nation, founded on a constitution, separating Church and State, was not allowed to

---

[1]  'The Anabaptist Vision', in *The Recovery of the Anabaptist Vision*, Ed. Guy S. Hershberger, Scottdale, Herald Press, 1957.

compromise the Mennonite prophetic stance to the Lordship of Jesus Christ, with its consequent commitment to social justice.[2]

Such Mennonite witness increasingly broke down academic hostility, enabling Mennonite scholars gradually to take their place on the world stage. Bender's views were supplanted by the work of three academics who proposed the multi-locational origins of the Anabaptist stream of radical Christianity.[3] We have briefly surveyed these three-plus roots is in the earlier '*Roots*' chapter.

This multi-rooted beginning (or 'polygenesis' as it was termed academically) strengthened the credibility of the vision behind all historic and contemporary Anabaptist witness. It demonstrated that in several European locations, radical Christian groups independently came to remarkably similar conclusions about their ongoing reaction to the nature of the Christendom Church. The perspective of Christian faith attributes this to the outworking (again) of the Holy Spirit. For evangelical Christians, this affirmed that the Anabaptist vision and witness must be God-given. Those with a more liberal theology recognize another community historically re-discerning biblical themes of liberation and working them out in community. This ability to gain approval across the Christian spectrum is an obvious outworking of being a visionary movement which is '*neither Protestant nor Catholic*'.

---

2

*Building Communities of Compassion,* Eds. William M. Swartley & Donald B. Kraybill, Scottdale, Herald Press,1998.

3

'From Monogenesis to Polygenesis: the Historical Discussion of Anabaptist Origins', James Stayer, Werner Packull, Klaus Deppermann, *Mennonite Quarterly Review*, 49, April 1975.

The photogenic qualities of both Amish and Hutterite life made them natural objects of both domestic tourism and *National Geographic* style features. In a world of space travel and sophistication, the vast majority of educated Americans wondered at and questioned what kind of vision could hold people in lives of seeming agrarian simplicity, without electricity, cars, phones and even zip fasteners. The film *Witness* (mentioned previously) and the growing global search for ethnic furnishing, be it Shaker furniture, Indian dhurries or Amish quilts, helped raise the international profile of Anabaptist groups and values. The north American chain of Mennonite-inspired franchise '*Ten Thousand Villages*' stores, selling such ethnic and other fair-trade goods, has helped raise the vision and profile of a 'just living', earth-friendly people.

Some of those who had dropped out in the 1960s Haight-Ashbury/hippy/Woodstock era dropped back into valuing such visionary communitarian examples, whether for academic study,[4] personal odyssey[5] or new styles of shared congregational households.[6]. The breadth of vision given by generations, if not centuries, of such Anabaptist communities provided one inspiration alongside others, for many young Americans seeking an alternative pattern to that of their parents.

---

[4]  *The Joyful Community,* Benjamin Zablocki, Chicago, UCP, 1971.

[5]  *Getting Back Together,* Robert Houriet, London, Abacus Press, 1975.

[6]  *Glimpses of Glory: Thirty Years of Reba Place Fellowship,* Dave & Neta Jackson, Elgin, Brethren Press, 1987.

Just a few years ago, I met a couple shopping in a *Ten Thousand Villages* store, in New Jersey; they seemed familiar. As we talked, we realized that we had camped next to each other, over thirty years before, at an early Glastonbury festival, in England. For us all, the hippy idealism of youth had not only translated continents but moved into the active support of a religious, namely Mennonite-inspired vision, still working for change.

Across postwar Europe, many young Mennonite volunteers worked in projects of reconciliation, youth mentoring, peace-making and community-building. Centres were funded jointly between indigenous Anabaptists and American Mennonites; the successive individuals who staffed these centres having a disproportionately large influence on both individuals and the surrounding, wider Christian community.

In north London, the work of John and Eileen Coffman in the student hostel, which later became the London Mennonite Centre, is still revered. Their leadership and later that of Alan and Eleanor Kreider (as LMC's Directors) helped create both the climate and individual openness which led to the formation of the UK and Ireland's now influential Anabaptist Network. Personally, I know of many individuals whose committed Anabaptist vision for life was formulated through the personal mentoring of the Coffmans and/or the Kreiders.

In the theological world, Anabaptism now has an increasing credibility. Historically, its early leaders were so quickly martyred that the opportunity for them to write extensively was limited; however those like Hubmaier, Marpeck and Simons wrote far more than only the tracts which others could manage. Hubmaier's *Articles of Faith*, used in the Peasants War struggle, and Sattler's drafting of the influential

*Schleitheim Confession* are now academically recognised as significantly shaping their relevant movements.

Presently, many Anabaptist theologians focus on particular topics for detailed exploration, such as J. Denny Weaver on 'atonement',[7] or Wilbert Shenk on 'mission'.[8] Alongside them, James Reimer[9] and more recently Thomas Finger[10] have effectively written well-received systematic theologies. But it is the multi-faceted work of John Howard Yoder[11] in the 20th century's last quarter that has most challenged world Christianity; several of his works have already been cited as footnotes.

Yoder, a Mennonite, held a professorship in the Roman Catholic Notre Dame University, sealing his reputation with the seminal book *The Politics of Jesus '*,[12] four books of visionary theological essays and lecturing on pacifism at the US's West Point military academy on the basis of his 1984 book *When War*

---

[7] *The Nonviolent Atonement,* J. Denny Weaver, Grand Rapids, Eerdmans, 2001.

[8] *The Transfiguration of Mission*, Ed. Wilbert Shenk, Scottdale, Herald Press,1993.

[9] *Mennonites and Classical Theology,* A. James Reimer, Ontario, Pandora Press, 2001.

[10] *A Contemporary Anabaptist Theology,* Thomas N. Finger, Downers Grove, IVP, 2004.

[11] *John Howard Yoder: Mennonite Patience, Evangelical Witness, Catholic Convictions,* Mark Thiessen Nation, Grand Rapids, Eerdmans, 2006.

[12] *The Politics of Jesus,* John Howard Yoder, Grand Rapids, Eerdmans, 1994 revision.

*is Unjust.*[13] Yoder's influence has been immense, providing the theological matrix upon which world renowned theologians such as Stanley Hauerwas[14] and James William McClendon particularly in his three volume Systematic Theology,[15] helping shape much early 21st century theology. Yet Yoder's adult life began as one of those postwar Mennonite volunteers, working in France 'wrangling horses', marrying a French woman before engaging in world-class academia.

At a global 'street level', Anabaptist witness is growing. As in the UK and Ireland, there is a growing Australia/New Zealand Anabaptist Network. In Scandinavia and Spain, there are also developing networks of Anabaptist groups and congregations, sitting alongside the older Alsatian and Russian Mennonite groupings and the city-based centres, such as Paris Seoul and London. Recently, Neal Blough, the director of the Paris Mennonite Centre, received a national French citation, naming him as one of the ten most influential Protestants. In SE Asia, the fastest growing Christian movement, alongside Pentecostalism, is Anabaptist–Mennonite in style and practice.

This points to the cogency with which the Anabaptist voice and vision can speak across cultures and countries where previously it has had no historic foothold. In the West, most numerical growth is due to those who find the coherence of the Anabaptist vision more relevant for their daily discipleship than

13
    *The Politics of Jesus,* John Howard Yoder, Maryknoll NY, Orbis, 1984; revised 1996.

14
    *Resident Aliens*, Stanley Hauerwas, & William H. Willimon, Nashville, Abingdon Press, 1989.

15
    *Systematic Theology, I, II & III*, James McClendon, Nashville, Abingdon Press, 1986, 1994 & 2000.

that of their former tradition; whereas in east and southern Asia the majority of growth is of those who are newly converted according to mission workers returning from those regions.

That vision is not merely spiritual but political, working from neighbourhood and city[16] to national and international levels.[17] Political in an Anabaptist context means the 'polis', that is of the people, creating an alternative philosophy of culture, community and involvement to which we return later in this chapter.

### SPIRITUALITY

This latter situation points to the innate spirituality of Anabaptist Jesus-centred discipleship. There will be those who argue that surely all Christianity is Jesus-centred. It is not – because patently Christianity is what it says – it is about 'following the Christ' figure. Regrettably 2000 years of Church history and 1500 years of European Christendom have done much to change the 'Jesus of history' into the 'Christ of the Church'. At a recent conference, I was publicly debating this with a Roman Catholic university lecturer who retorted to my argument "...*but Holy Mother Church teaches*". Anabaptism tolerates no such intermediary between the individual disciple and the God-whom-we-know-in-Jesus.

However, Anabaptism recognises that the congregation collectively shares in the discipling responsibilities. Congregations may federate into local, regional, even national

---

16      *Artists, Citizens, Philosophers,* Duane K. Friesen, Scottdale, Herald Press, 2000.

17      *For the Nations*, John Howard Yoder, Grand Rapids, Eerdmans, 1997.

forms of association, but the relationship created is non-hierarchical and any/every statement or ruling has to be consensually agreed by either the whole body or congregational representatives nominated to speak on behalf of the local group. Spiritual authority is about love and influence rather than the exercise of physical power.

This echoes Jesus' teaching and stance, even towards his executioners, in the ongoing life and spirituality of Anabaptist communities and congregations. Jesus own yielding to his killers set the practice of *Gelassenheit* into Anabaptist discipleship and it it this 'yieldedness' which underpins an individual's submission to congregational discipline.

Traditionally, Anabaptist congregations have chosen unanimously, and members agree on joining, to be subject to collective discipling on the basis of Matthew 18 vv.15–18; historically this was known as 'the ban'. Yet even when an individual was shunned following an individual act of a corporately acknowledged transgression, as soon as repentance was professed and forgiveness declared, the act of wrongdoing was never publicly spoken of again, nor held against the individual. Regrettably, this practice of 'the ban' seeming an ideal way to exercise Christian discipline, it is (and often has been) open to misuse; sadly this is sufficiently recognised to have spilled into popular fiction.[18]

The pattern for Anabaptist discipleship should always be set by the Jesus of the Gospels. Therefore Anabaptist–style spirituality will be modelled by Jesus himself. In the Gospels we discover a Jesus who relishes personal prayer, a rootedness in the scriptures, who worships in the neighbourhood

[18]    *Plain Truth,* Jodi Picoult, London, Flame, 2004.

community (for Jesus, this was the synagogue) and whose significant others is a small group of his disciples. Jesus taught *'Whoever does the will of my Father in heaven, is my sister, my brother...'* (Matthew 12 vv.48–50) indicating that our own small discipleship group is at least as significant for our practice of faith and spirituality as that of our earthly, blood family – if not more so.

Historically song and personal testimony have been pillars of Anabaptist spirituality. Small groups of Anabaptists awaiting martyrdom would exhort each other with hymns of faith (collected together in a volume called the *Ausbund*) and with their own testimonies and those of preceding martyrs. Contemporary Anabaptists hardly ever gather without singing or sharing their own stories to encourage one another. Equally now, the gathering of small groups, often sharing food, is vital for the conversational interchange of ideas and vision as well as mutually correcting patterns of discipleship.

Anabaptists happily engage with other Christians. Historically, some Anabaptists were heavily influenced by the Rhineland Mystics, particularly the spirituality of Johannes Tauler.[19] We have already referred to Anabaptists being described as *'neither Protestant nor Catholic'*. Presently, in the UK, most Anabaptists began their Christian journey elsewhere but continue to retain their denominational allegiances for the sake of retaining a wide level of Christian fellowship. Ecumenical openness is a mark of contemporary Anabaptist witness.

---

[19]    *Mysticism and the South German–Austrian Anabaptist Movement.* Werner Packull, Scottdale, Herald Press, 1977.

My first encounter with a live Mennonite (a Canadian) was at the ecumenical Taizé Community in France, whilst still a teenager; she was far more accepting of candles, multi-lingual chant and liturgy than I was. Anabaptism is sufficiently comfortable in its skin to draw from the richness and liturgy of other traditions; this is very apparent in the recently published Anabaptist Prayer book with its daily services: '*Take our Moments and our Days*'.[20] Equally, amongst the resources I suggest to newly forming Anabaptist groups is Sara Wenger Shenk's *Why Not Celebrate?*,[21] which again draws on a global and historic breadth of Christian spirituality.

But always the touchstone is Jesus and his way of being. Daily prayer is the beating heart of discipleship. Familiarity with the Christian scriptures, particularly the Gospel testimonies of Jesus, is the life-shaping pattern.[22] A local congregation, which is mutually accountable to one another, is best able to become the Christian community in which worship, mission and service can be shared. Being part of a small, frequently meeting discipleship group can become the anvil upon which mature vision and spirituality is forged. This echoes Jesus' own example and is the pattern of nearly all the committed Anabaptist-Christians of my acquaintance.

---

[20]    Eds. Boers, Gingerich, Kreider, Rempel & Schertz, Scottdale, Herald Press, 2007.

[21]    Pub. Intercourse, Good Books, 1987.

[22]    *Biblical Interpretation in the Anabaptist Tradition,* Stuart Murray, Ontario, Pandora Press, 2000.

### COMMUNITY

The biblical witness of Acts chapters 2 and 4 is that at least some Christians lived in community, sharing homes and possessions, because of the expected imminent return of Jesus and the End-time. Yet the witness of the Desert Fathers, through medieval monasticism to contemporary movements such of those of the Iona, Taizé, Focolare, Waldensian and various other post-modern Celtic communities demonstrate that community is at the heart of some ongoing stream of biblical interpretation for corporate discipleship.

In 2009, the UK's Anabaptist Network jointly held an well-attended conference on the 'New Monasticism' with the Northumbria Community. The numbers of those seeking a radical spirituality which is coherently woven into a network-but-dispersed community is growing.

The 16th century, and subsequent, persecution of Anabaptism created its communitarian streams. Those who were driven into Moravia, where their hard work and simple lifestyle afforded them the protection of the local feudal lord, offer examples for our future. For such historic groups, there remains an open question whether it was 'safety in numbers' or biblical example that caused them to live communally. In those western European neighbourhoods, where antagonism to Christian hypocrisy is growing, the rediscovery and adoption of Anabaptist patterns of community could become an alternative vibrant Christian witness; examples are offered later in this chapter.

We have already referred to those extended household groups such as the Hutterites, and the Bruderhofs. Around 1700, from Bruderhof beginings, a separatist Swiss group gathering communally around Jakob Ammann evolved whilst migrating towards north America into the Amish.

The Nazi purges of the mid 20th century drove the German Bruderhof into exile both in south America and the English Cotswolds; this latter group is still extant in three Bruderhof communities, one in Robertsbridge–Sussex, another in Nonington–Kent (both now have far less emphasis on agriculture as their means of support), and a small inner London community house. Sadly the Bruderhof leadership appear increasingly ambivalent to their Anabaptist heritage when interest in historic communitarian Anabaptism is alive and well today, with the biggest conglomeration being the various Amish or 'Plain people' (*on account of their plain style of dress*) groups in Pennsylvania, USA.[23]

However a majority of Anabaptists today live in some form of 'dispersed community'. This normally is created around the 'congregation-as-community' ethos and the desire for a sustainable, simple lifestyle. Much of western Christendom and traditional denominationalism is built around 'Sunday church-going', assuming that churchgoers utilize their innate Christian values for the business of all other living. Falling church attendances and the increasing secularity of western Europe shows how (un)workable that Christendom model is. Anabaptist Christians and congregations seek to offer an alternative practice.

It is easy to over-idealise the pattern of Anabaptist congregational life, as they attempt to be more localised, enabling most members to walk to Sunday worship and midweek gatherings as well as each other's homes. Congregations are seedbeds of sharing – not just of meals but

---

23   *The Puzzles of Amish Life*, Donald B. Kraybill, Intercourse, Good Books, 1998.

everyday tools, excess furniture and vehicles.[24] Whilst visiting one congregation, I was naturally asked to walk a lawnmower to my tea-time hosts *"just two blocks away"* as it was their evening to use it.

Congregations often form work-parties to help decorate older members' homes and help prepare or refurbish property for new owners. The money so liberated can help individual congregations support their own students, between college courses, to undertake voluntary work elsewhere in the world. Eating together is a mark of most Anabaptist Sunday congregational gatherings and of nearly all midweek (home-based) groups for prayer and Bible study.[25] Families will often buy larger, older, relatively less expensive properties and take in single members of the congregation, sometimes adapting homes for multi-occupancy.

The sharing of goods and vehicles as well as homes builds up a rich network of relationships within a congregation, creating a sense of extended family as well as community. Some congregations such Evanston's Reba Place (mentioned earlier) and others have a long pedigree of deliberately using shared households as part of their Christian witness and mission.[26] Sometimes these communities are intentionally short-lived.

In the late 1970s/1980s Hull, a group of postgraduate Christians chose to live closely together in four households in

[24]  *Living More With Less,* Doris Janzen Longacre, Scottdale, Herald Press, 1980.

[25]  *The Best of Mennonite Fellowship Meals,* Ed. Phyllis Pellman Good, Scottdale, Herald Press,1985.

[26]  *Living in Christian Community,* Art Gish, Sidney, Albatross Books, 1980.

neighbouring streets, for their final years of study. This group ate together in their households daily, met twice weekly for worship and a meal, shared two washing machines, one minibus, lots of bikes and two small cars and each undertook some local voluntary work. All this helped build both theirs and the surrounding community as well as witness to their faith – which was Anabaptist in style if not in name. They had all chosen to be (re-)baptised as believers, lent me my first full copy of Yoder's *Politics of Jesus*, and introduce me to other Anabaptist books.

In Northampton, a group of Christians (including some who were part of the Anabaptist Network) have bought adjoining terraced homes, sharing gardens and white goods, calling themselves 'The Neighbours'; several of them also work in the local *'Daily Bread'* co-operative bakery. In the surrounding county, the Jesus Army is based in Bugbrooke Manor and over twenty other communal households.[27]

Importantly, 'the neighbours' do not define themselves as an Anabaptist community, whereas the Jesus Army have discovered that their biblical discernment for community and believers' baptism sets them firmly in the pattern of the Anabaptist tradition, whilst their alleged fundamentalist theology would not.

As in the earlier Bruderhof ambivalence, these two further examples raise an important principle about what it means to be an Anabaptist. How much 'reading back', adoption or retro-fitting is permissible to call a group 'Anabaptist', whilst asking is it even possible to deny a heritage or tradition

[27]    *Fire in our Hearts,* Simon Cooper & Mike Farrant, Brighton, Kingsway, 1991.

by ignoring it, particularly if the group involved still practices some of its central distinctive tenets.

In north London, the Wood Green Mennonite Church still wrestles with the vision of whether they could buy houses closer to each other to become more of a localised witness as a 'dispersed community'. However, not all Anabaptist Christians are within sensible geographical reach of such types of congregation and seek alternative ways of being community. Successively over more than twenty-five years, in Leeds, Kent, France and Wiltshire, I have sought to be part of a small fortnightly Anabaptist-style home-based group which meets for a meal, discussion and prayer/Bible-study.

Within the UK, the Anabaptist Network has encouraged the development of regional study groups; a few meet monthly, whilst other meet less frequently, some sharing a similar meal–discussion–prayer pattern, thus potentially creating community for radical Christians. Some of these groups particularly in the West Midlands and Yorkshire have developed a sufficient frequency of meeting, as well as numbers, that they have become dispersed communities or congregations in all but name. What must be acknowledged is that the strength of these groups *may* be short-lived and that there is no consistency or nationwide pattern of response.

PRACTICAL ACTION

Most of my highly activist Anabaptist friends have two particular books on their shelves; one is Yoders' *The Politics of Jesus*, and the other is one of the versions of a popular Mennonite cookbook.[28] Rather than support this anecdotally,

---

[28]   *More-With-Less Cookbook,* Doris Jansen Longacre, Scottdale, Herald Press, 1976.

the sales figures of the radical *Metanoia* book service and Stuart Murray's book, *The Naked Anabaptist*, also confirm this. This tells something of the trajectory of Anabaptist-flavoured discipleship: it is built around practical action, declaring Jesus is Lord of every part of life, and sharing meals together. I rejoice in the phrase *'Shalom Activism'*. The practical outworking of faith is the way that others discern the nature of the presence of vibrant Christian discipleship. Many small UK Anabaptist groups have a particular emphasis on their life together.

For several years, one such Black Country group was led by a couple whose tiny terraced home was packed with *Traidcraft goods.*[29] Together the group promoted the sale of fair-trade goods within many local congregations, in their own work-places, running stalls at day conferences and speaking in schools – all sharing the workload. Another couple used their work-related visits to India to buy local craft goods, parcelling them back to the UK where they re-sold them, using the profits to fund co-operative enterprises back in India.

Another Worcestershire based group, *Wildfire,* spent five years re-developing a set of farm buildings into eight eco-homes, each unit with its own allotment and solar heating panels, but sharing one reedbed sewage system. Conversation with their leadership team in 1996 revealed their acknowledgement of and debt to historic Anabaptism and contemporary Mennonite projects as key influences. At least one of *Wildfire's* leaders is now heavily involved in the UK's Christian Ecology Link.

[29]    www.traidcraft.co.uk

In both Manchester and Leeds respectively, committed Anabaptist couples began Greenpeace and Amnesty International cells. Now using cyber social media, such as Facebook groups, Anabaptists are often founding specific campaigning groups and/or encountering one another through such media usage. In each of these cases it was the Anabaptist committment to practical action which drove the founding motivation – this was explicitly acknowledged and evoked interest, sometimes commitment, to the movement in others. Today's Anabaptists have been quick to recognize that the activist cell, targeting specific issues in Jesus-centred ways, both creates strong, viable witness and gets results – and it may not need to last forever.

Anabaptists involved in such activities do not differ from other Christians who are also active in such ways, there just seem to be more of them relatively. Unlike more traditional denominational Christianity, Anabaptists seem to be more prepared to take the direct route as well as accepting that a project or piece of practical action may only have a short lifespan. Over thirty years ago, my own and another household ran a simple food co-operative, bulk buying flour, pulses and honey then selling on in smaller quantities to friends. What is vital is that the values (or core practices as identified in the previous chapter) are expounded in simple, clear action and lifestyle.

Many Anabaptists of my acquaintance can recount several examples when friends and neighbours have been astonished by the level of Anabaptists' co-operation and sharing. Particular examples have involved not just the sharing of vehicles, large tools and furniture but of skills when help regularly arrives for decorating, building and gardening projects. I hardly know an Anabaptist who is not a registered 'freecycler', committed fair-trade supporter and active household recycler; many have allotments and bikes, and even flat-dwellers have pots of herbs or tomatoes on balconies or in window-boxes. Obviously, other Christians *do* become involved in all these activities and although these practical emphases are not essentials of Anabaptist belief, they are often essentials of a life style which is openly declared to be that of the Anabaptist-Christian.

Clearly such activism has a green/eco tinge. This is about the whole household of God – it is a pattern of *oikemene* (ecumenical activity), which is about being earth-centred, accepting responsibility as a global citizen. '*Think global – act local'* is a very Anabaptist maxim. In north America, over several decades, the Mennonites have funded a variety of 'green projects' to provide education and model what is possible for others to do.[30] The London Mennonite Centre has recently considered a number of options for a small pilot eco-project to use part of its garden. Again, these collective responses cannot be claimed as exclusively Anabaptist, or even Christian, but for a movement with some historic roots in agrarian exile, its trajectory and theology of global cognisance means that contemporary eco/planetary concerns form a natural part of the movement's agenda.

Institutionally, such places as the London Mennonite Centre have become seedbeds for sharing Anabaptist values, in starting then supporting new projects which are nurtured towards their own independence. Its *Metanoia* internet book

[30]     *Earthkeepers,* Art & Jocele Meyer, Scottdale, Herald Press, 1991.

service[31] has been influential in supplying books encouraging radical discipleship and lifestyle, of Anabaptist theology, peace-making and congregational development. Previous reference has been made to the LMC starting and nurturing the now nationally respected and self-financing conflict mediation service, *Bridge Builders;*[32] through its specialist courses, it trains conflict mediators, including nearly all those who are called to serve as regional leaders of most English denominations.

This use of specific skills is utilized by many individual Anabaptists who serve in particular, voluntary leadership roles in their local communities. Many choose to become school governors or parish councillors. The historic injunction against Anabaptists serving as magistrates in case they have to inflict violent, or even capital, punishment pertains sufficiently that most UK Anabaptists (like me!) still choose to refuse such nomination 'to the Bench'. However, I much more readily serve as a member of (and often chair) NHS Mental Health Appeal Panels, accepting that this judicial process is about ensuring justice and 'fair process' for those checking their personal detention under statute within psychiatric units. Others often choose to serve as trustees or in the local management of particular charities.

Serving the needs of others is central to Anabaptist practical action. However, it is entirely appropriate to question how Anabaptists involved in such activities differ from other Christians who are also active in such ways?

---

[31]     www.menno.org.uk/metanoia

[32]     www.bridgebuilders.co.uk

Increasingly, Anabaptists are making both life and career choices to enable practical action, for the benefit of others, to be central to their lives. Typically those of us who have been privileged to serve in the national Anabaptist Network's Steering Group or speak frequently at conferences, build our own large web of Anabaptist contacts across the country. Often, just as in our 16<sup>th</sup> century history, my contacts may not be known to all the other Steering Group members; the element of quiet local discipleship continues to mark the nature of the movement. Anabaptists used to be known as *'the quiet in the land'.*

It is typically Anabaptist that no one individual ever knows the spread and involvement, practical or otherwise, of the whole movement. That has many strengths. One is that we tend to ask around, by phone and email, to find someone involved in what we need to discover more about. In turn this is building the network informally and strengthening links/relationships between like-minded Anabaptist-Christians to work for social and spiritual change. At the end of this book, there is a series of thumbnail sketches of some of my Anabaptist contacts illustrating the movement's 'reach' and breadth.

#### BUT IS IT ANABAPTISM?

When is something part of the movement and when is it not? How far back in the movement must influence be evidenced to say this is Anabaptist? Or how much 'external' influence is permissible before something is just Anabaptist orientated rather than simply Anabaptist?

Most contemporary Anglican theology is built upon the work of Richard Hooker (1554–1600), setting out the three–fold premise of 'Scripture – Tradition – Reason', yet I have Anglo–Catholic acquaintances who joyfully leapfrog Hooker backwards to claim that Henry VIII's English Catholic

Church was *"much better"* than Hooker's model. At an ecumenical conference, I heard a former President of the Methodist Conference quietly disabuse a fellow Methodist who claimed "We're all with Mr. Wesley on this"; they were not according to this esteemed Methodist leader.

So does every Anabaptist have to trace their practical discipleship back to Schleitheim in 1527 for it to be legitimately explored as genuinely Anabaptist? At what point can later, and possible external, influences be properly determinative within the movement's practices and discipleship? It is both important and right to question when something has been properly adopted into the (or any) movement and when something is being retro–fitted.

For example, I keep on file newspaper articles from *The Times*, and others, in 2000 (and onwards), attributing Amish agricultural practice as decisively influencing the 'back–to–the–land' movement. Obviously not all 'greens' and 'eco–warriors' are Anabaptists, but if this is what drew them to the movement, at what point can it be claimed to be *not* part of historic Anabaptist discipleship? Some years ago, when visiting the Greenham Common protestors, they were passing around Mennonite books on peace-making. The movement's influence, because of its principles and core practices, has been broad. It is appropriate to exercise critique of what is Anabaptist and not.

Anabaptist thought can never fully agree with contemporary liberal and philosophical ideas that the 'freedom of the individual' is paramount. Anabaptist thought and theology always insist that 'the concept of community' (in its various understandings) is also considered. Such two-fold thinking is not typical of all or across-the-board Christian theology. Therefore, how an individual Anabaptist chooses to serve local society must be in a role which benefits the whole, that is everyone, without it being to the potential detriment of any one individual.

Certainly there are issues to which Anabaptists bring a distinctive voice, with specific insights and emphasis. In the 'strange bedfellows' alliances which some of these issues create for campaigners, it should be noted that other, perhaps more expert, voices bring their agendas too.

**SUMMARY**

Exemplifying these four principles (vision, spirituality, community, practical action) can give an extremely optimistic view of this radical Christian movement, which is tiny in these islands compared to the size and spread of many of the traditional denominations. Personally, I find that optimism helpful. Having served as a United Reformed Church minister for over twenty–five years in several contexts (from inner-city through suburbia to market-town), I recognize that UK Christianity is involved in a real struggle to engage in mission. To be involved in a movement, which has a more radical approach to its vision, the expression of spirituality, its understanding of community and its commitment to practical action, is not just encouraging but life-giving.

Anabaptists are people of principle, who respect the right and conscience of all but particularly those who use faith principles to determine their life and activity. Anabaptists naturally witness to their faith; the guy on the next allotment can look rather envious when all your local group turn up to do the digging and weeding, inevitably asking his questions...

We now turn to the final chapter which invites you, the reader, to consider some of the the personal challenges of Anabaptism.

# Taking up the challenge...

Some years ago, I took up the Yorkshire Three Peaks Challenge on an amazingly clear summer's day. Our small group followed that year's advocated route (to prevent undue erosion), and walked nearly thirty miles. As we were reaching the top of the second peak (Whernside), we could look back at the previous peak and look ahead to the terrain before the next one. Each peak achieved afforded us a different view of the surrounding landscape.

Radical discipleship, as several of my Quaker and Anabaptist friends often remind me, is like that: there is always another peak to be achieved, and you do get a different view of the surrounding 'landscape'. It requires discipline and commitment to keep going and that is most easily achieved with a small group of similarly dedicated others.

Anabaptism is no God-of-the-gaps agenda; it speaks to the whole of life, rather than just the inexplicable bits. It has a vibrant and vital voice to bring to the discernment and decisive conversations surrounding many contemporary issues. These next few pages highlight just five of those issues to encourage you to recognise the challenge – then look at the surrounding landscape, political and theological, from each of those viewpoints.

Again it must be noted that none of these issues are *exclusively* Anabaptist concerns. Certainly they are issues to which Anabaptists bring their distinctive voice...

### CHURCH AND STATE

How long can the Church, and particularly the Church of England and the Church of Scotland, go on claiming privileged places in 21st century British society? Church-going has been in decline since the early 20th century.[1] How many populist media surveys, showing how few children know the Lord's Prayer or young people know what Easter's meaning is, will it take for an introspective Church to. properly and continually question its own modus operandi?

The case for Disestablishment (that is, severing the formal ties between Church and State) grows increasingly stronger across Britain.[2] France broke such ties in 1912 and, despite fears, Catholic witness has continued, but the resultant pluralism has allowed more independent churches to operate on an equal level. The United States have used their Constitution to enable religious liberty (helping Amish, Mennonites and other Anabaptists to develop their own patterns of shared discipleship), yet their dollars proclaim *'In God we trust'* and Presidents intone *'God bless America'*. Separating Church and State can never squeeze God out of society.

Why should certain Anglican bishops continue to sit in the House of Lords as of right, when far more Christians and other people *choose* not to be Anglicans? What have the organized denominations to fear? If the British Government is serious about both its pluralist and politically correct agenda, it is anachronistic to maintain the privileged rights of one religious grouping over many others, whatever our history.

[1]  *Under God's Good Hand,* p110, David Cornick, London, URC Press, 1988.

[2]  *Church and State: Uneasy Alliances,* Stewart Lamont, London, The Bodley Head, 1989.

Such privileges are a mark of a vestigial Christendom.[3] Bring on Disestablishment. Let those cathedrals which have historic, architectural merit receive grants in similar competition to other noteworthy buildings and grand houses. Let individual churches and denominations be judged by the same criteria as all other charities, to see if they deserve charitable status *before* giving them tax-breaks.

In arguing to retain a privileged position, 'the Church' remains aloof whilst appearing both supercilious and 'holier-than-thou'. That was not the kind of egalitarian community that Jesus nurtured, in which all are welcomed as equals. Over the past five centuries, Jesus' Anabaptist flavoured disciples have been a *Bundschuh* movement of the people, often shunning wealth, position and rank, to witness to their Saviour's example. So, if 'the Church' could acknowledge the flaws and imperialism of its Christendom past, it might not remain the butt of so much humour. Also, it might diminish the alienation so many experience and lessen the radicalization of youth who then adopt patterns of violence, terrorism or crime.

Anabaptists do not support a Christendom mentality, with its attendant rights and privileges. Their egalitarian approach advocates religious tolerance and the right to exercise faith in whatever manner – providing it does not cause harm or offence to others – for the good of the whole society and the benefit of all God's creation.

### FAITH AND SCHOOLS

Those of us who are old enough to remember the troubles in Ulster during the 1960s and '1970s, can recall the

---

[3]   *Post Christendom,* Stuart Murray, Carlisle, Paternoster, 2004.

frightening scenes of primary school children being escorted to school by armed soldiers; this was because they were Protestants walking through Catholic neighbourhoods or vice-versa. Since then, similar occurrences have been witnessed by Jewish and Palestinian children in Israel and the Occupied Territories; 9/11 and increasing radicalization of Islamic youth are reminders of the damage caused when western imperialism and sectarianism coincide.

Any argument about education and equal justice, which Anabaptists naturally support, would mean that if the State chooses both to allow and financially support Anglican and Catholic faith-based schools, then that similar privilege ought to be accorded to Jewish and Islamic day schools, too; this is both logical and natural justice.

However, the lessons of Ulster, the Palestinian Occupied Territories, 9/11 and the simmering tensions of some English inner cities, with their particular faith-based enclaves, provide lessons which our wider society ignores at its peril. How long will it be before a primary school in West Yorkshire, the Midlands or London, suggests that because it has only (or a 95% majority of) children from Muslim families its discipline should be based upon sharia law or that all teaching could be conducted in Arabic? There would be outrage if some state-supported Jewish schools taught everything, from maths to geography, only in Hebrew. Consistency and justice are needed.

If the UK Government persists in a pluralist agenda, it must include integration within schools and active policies to close sectarian faith-based, State-supported schools. It is disgraceful that some UK denominations are committed to supporting supposedly ecumenical church schools, perpetrating both further divisions in the wider society and reasons to allow ongoing sectarian education. Church leaders often defend the 'church schools' privilege on the basis of such schools' popularity because they have better disciplinary records or higher moral standards. Perhaps! But did not Jesus invite his followers to become *'the leaven in the lump'* thus working to change the whole of society to Jesus' values rather than withdraw into a privileged part of it?

Most school governors of my acquaintance, share increasing concern at the legal requirement to ensure that *"all pupils in attendance at a maintained school shall on each school day take part in an act of collective worship ...* (which) *shall be wholly or mainly of a broadly Christian character."*[4] Despite legal caveats allowing the separation of year groups and other consultative factors, most school governors and head teachers know it is hard to find enough Christians on the staff to daily lead this, as well as impossible to easily timetable this. Virtually every reader will have anecdotal evidence why such school assemblies should be led only by committed Christians. Anabaptists, like most thinking Christian, Jewish, and Muslim believers, would far prefer that worship is held within the 'faith communities' rather than imposed upon children in the school environment, particularly when it is led by non-believers.

I do not know an Anabaptist who would not support major political change which removes daily religious assemblies, for collective worship, from State-supported schools as well as removing the right of whatever faith-group to effectively control the style and delivery of State-supported schools.

---

[4]     UK Education Reform Act, 1988, Section 6.

## THE ECONOLOGICAL DISCUSSION

In their traditional acceptance of 'community of goods' as a very normal part of life (whether living in a shared household or not), Anabaptists have demonstrated Jesus' own teaching (*'If anyone has two coats, let him give one...'*) and the biblical patterns of community, shown in early chapters of Acts (2, 4, 5 and 16). Such sharing is also replicated in much current Anabaptist concern for ecology and the planetary footprints of every individual, in seeking to use no more natural resources than really needed.

A previous chapter has already alluded to this practical and theological concern for the whole of God's earth. The Greek word *'oikos'* referred to then, meaning 'household', is the root of English words such as 'ecumenical', 'economical' and 'ecological'. Whatever the exact scientific view of climate change, the necessary responses have both economic and ecological impacts. Now, the growing use of the blended word 'econological', by serious broadcast media as well as in books and journals, is a reminder of the broader implications that any and every response will affect us all widely.

This short book began with the idea that 'witness' is central to the nature of Anabaptist life. In a few pages, there are some thumbnail sketches of (some of my) Anabaptist friends. Many of them have positively chosen to 'downshift,'[5] electing a simpler life, lower income, often smaller houses and fewer material possessions and adopting an earth-friendly lifestyle. Few would use the word 'econological' but acknowledge their chosen life-changes have given them far more than economic

5 *Downshifting: the Guide to Simpler, Happier Living,* Polly Ghazi & Judy Jones, London, Coronet, 1997.

benefits and the planet some ecological benefits. But their daily example, in other words their witness, of simple Jesus-style living tells its story. When the elderly neighbour of one Anabaptist acquaintance sold her home, a Quaker family bought it because they liked what they saw of the "next-door folk who grew runner beans in the front garden and had a peace symbol in the front window". Every picture tells a story.

But we need to see the big picture too. It was Mennonite inspiration which led to the publication of the well-received *Christianity and the Culture of Economics,*[6] which I have heard used in regional political exchange and serious BBC Radio 4 debate. Among other Christians, Anabaptists offered key chapters on shareholder values, workers' co-operatives and Amish economics. Patterns of economic co-operation in and beyond both the workplace and home are a natural expression of Anabaptism and biblical teaching. *'Living simply that others may simply live'* is not just a maxim but increasingly a necessity.

This becomes even more apparent when the needs of the world are considered. Simply the way in which we eat needs to be a matter of thought, not just a matter of blindly ticking off the family list at the supermarket. Everyone in my local Anabaptist group was shocked when we passed around a photocopied (yes, I know) quiz to check our personal and domestic carbon footprints. Now each one of us is making some significant change to our lifestyle – and talking about it to our friends and neighbours; again, this is 'witness'.

More widely, Anabaptists share with others both interest and commitment towards 'shared housing', co-housing

---

[6]    Donald A. Hay & Alan Kreider, Cardiff, University of Wales Press, 2001.

projects, eco-living and car-sharing schemes. Whilst many naturally look to other agencies, whether national eco-charities or local (allotment and other) groups, for 'green-thinking', they are pleasantly surprised that a radical Christian movement shares similar perspectives. Such thinking becomes even more important as consideration turns to the nature of the global community.

Perhaps one of the greatest challenges to western Anabaptists is that those whose planetary footprints sit well in the world are East Asian peasant families, who subsistence farm, and those in the near-East, such as Afghanis and Iraqis, who we, as a British nation, increasingly treat as our enemies. It is then that the Anabaptist stance on peace-making helps 'econology' become part of our joined-up thinking.

### PEACE-MAKING

Peace-making is a whole spectrum of both activity and attitude. Just as historic Anabaptists wrestled with whether to be 'sword-bearers', or even 'staff-bearers', contemporary Anabaptists range from the complete pacifist to those who accept the use of non-lethal force in the restraint of individuals and crowds.

In telling the story of the Good Samaritan, Jesus challenged the racial prejudice of his Jewish listeners in asking *'Who is my neighbour?'* In reminding his disciples to *'Go the extra mile.'* and *'Turn the other cheek.'* Jesus taught that we can challenge our oppressors and enemies by an unexpected non-violent response. These key texts for Anabaptists are a way of challenging both our own and others' prejudices, such as against those Afghanis and Iraqis.

Today's Anabaptists remain convinced that there is *no* such thing as a 'just war'. This doctrine was worked out in the Christendom era, with theologians such as Augustine and

Aquinas refining its definition. There are several pre-conditions for a conflict to be considered a 'just war'. One is that it is *'necessary and proportionate'*, and another that it is waged by legitimate authorities; there can be many arguments of principle about the nature of these two pre-conditions. However, another is that *'civilians must not be hurt nor become casualties of the conflict'*; there can be no argument that the carpet-bombings of Coventry and Dresden, as well as the atomization of central Hiroshima and Nagasaki, robbed these perpetrating nations of all moral authority and claims of just cause. Likewise, the pre-condition that the land must not be *"damaged for more than one harvest"* means that I question whether any British politician, who looks at post-WW1 Flanders fields (or any American politician who looks at ongoing Japanese deformities) can really say they have properly considered that the conflicts involved were 'just wars'.

Therefore contemporary Anabaptist witness seeks to foster debate about the 'just war', campaigns, forging alliances with other religious (e.g. Quakers) and secular (e.g. *Stop The War*) groups. What is little known is the Anabaptist involvement in groups helping the militarily bereaved, or supporting conscientious objections, as other facets of such peace-making ministry. Recall the fact that some like John Howard Yoder (whose authoritative book *When War is Unjust* should be required reading) regularly debated the issue at West Point military academy, enabling officer-cadets to recognize the strength of the counter-argument to their nation's assumed raison d'etre. When the Leeds Vickers' tank factory faced closure, the local Anabaptist group worked alongside others economically to lobby for alternative non-armaments-based employment instead.

In working for change, Anabaptists are having to be prepared to work at several levels to enable others to recognize that peace-making options can make sense – economically and employment-wise as well in the more global humanitarian concerns. As individuals, there has already been reference to those working in conflict mediation and Victim-Offender Reconciliation Programmes. Just like many other Christians, Anabaptist choose professional lives working in education, social work, community development and the charity sector; in everything, there is a desire to remove coercion from the agenda of such work. Those who criticize the complicity involved in acceptance of State employment often forget that this can provide opportunity to influence policy, whilst treating individuals with due care. In doing these things, there is both peace-making and witness.

### DYNAMIC DISCIPLESHIP

Just like climbing and hill walking, Anabaptists seldom adventure alone. The place of the small group has been important from the days of the Zurich radicals through to the work of the regional study groups of the Anabaptist Network today.

Anabaptists are not Sunday Christians, popping down to "8 o'clock Communion" or the later family service. Following after the way of Jesus (remember *Nachfolge*) is a matter of daily discipleship, meaning that sharing faith in Jesus affects the way we live, the jobs we do, our shopping and eating choices as well as the homes we live in. Being part of a small discipleship group enables discussion of those choices and priorities, as well as testing out other important life-choices. Anabaptists choose to yield as much of their selfish individualism (remember *Gelassenheit*) as possible to others' scrutiny. If distance precludes Sunday worship together, the monthly or fortnightly

Anabaptist cell assumes both high priority and great significance in Jesus-shaped living.

In chemistry terms, it is a form of dynamic equilibrium, with an ongoing two-way interchange of ideas between the individual and the group. Diagrammatically, it can be represented by the cross–dove logo from the front cover (reproduced by the kind permission of the London Mennonite Centre Trustees). The individual has chosen to conform his or her life to the cross-shaped example of Jesus but the nature of that is mediated through the Spirit-led counsel and support of the discipleship group. The interplay of Cross and Spirit enables each disciple to exercise their faith in ways consonant with that of the Jesus-shaped community, historic and contemporary, to which they belong.

Inevitably, this commitment to and through the discipleship community leads to an understanding of shared spirituality and vision, whilst naturally creating an accountability for each individual's practical outworking of their discipleship. Whilst such patterns are not unique to Anabaptism, it is not rocket science to recognize that the four defining principles (as explained in the last chapter) are dynamically embodied in each individual as well the discipleship group to which they belong. Just as there is interactivity between Cross and Spirit, so there is similar interactivity between the individual and the 'community of faith'.

Yet this interactivity is missional in orientation. It allows the non-believer to join a local group, provided they are open-minded enough to accept and learn the practice of prayer. Their assimilation into the group can often begin by sorting out Anabaptist behavioural patterns, such as peace-making, serving others daily in their own life. During that journey, the teachings and person of Jesus often come alive, allowing belief, then vibrant faith to follow. Understanding this possibly explains why Anabaptism is one of faster growing forms of Christianity in Asia. Perhaps, this is also why it is so feared by those western churches still rooted in the Christendom practice of solely Sunday congregations. Joining an Anabaptist group means risking the possibility of becoming a dynamic disciple of Jesus.

**THEREFORE**...

THINK GLOBAL – ACT LOCAL!

Anabaptism has stood the test of time and persecution, operating in many different cultures and regions of the world. The movement knows how to stand at the margins of society but offers a voice at society's heart on the big issues that matter. Yet it is those dispersed small groups of Anabaptist-flavoured Christians who, understanding the 'beat of the street', can help an individual to make sense of life, the universe and all that is beyond.

In contemporary Britain, the increasing fragmentation of society and local neighbourhoods, as well as family breakdown, is isolating more people. A radical Christian movement, built around local small-group discipleship rather than just offering 'Sunday solace' has much to commend it. Anabaptism is one such a movement, deserving serious attention and choice. This way of Christianity will not be for everyone (however regrettable that may be to me) because of its daily demands. Equally, there will always be those who dance to a different drum.

Anabaptist are fallible people, just like every other Christian. They do not share all the same views, party politics and faith ambitions. In company with many others, Anabaptists seek to build a better, more peaceable world in which all are fed, housed and respected. Unlike others who shout about the same or similar ideals, Anabaptists *try* to live out and speak the quiet words of Jesus who is both their saviour and example in life and in death and in resurrection. Alongside Quakers and other radical Christians, Anabaptists are part of a vanguard seeking to ensure ensure faith, discipleship and lifestyle are as one in each and every day and everyone's way of life.

**MEET SOME OF MY FRIENDS...**

All these folk have been heavily influenced by Anabaptism; some are very active in the movement, and known to each other, others less so. In some cases, I have used pseudonyms.

**Ann,** a Wiltshire craft worker, church administrator, bread maker, veg grower. Ann lives with her daughter and cat, reads prolifically, nurtures friendships and enjoys co-hosting her local group.

**Bill and Jane,** Hampshire downshifters, veg growers, wine makers. After Bill's heart surgery, they retreated to their small New Forest holiday home, letting their London City flat for income. Bill now advises independent charity shops in business practice whilst Jane runs a playgroup.

**David,** a Home-counties fair trade and justice campaigner, home-group leader, chief executive of international charity. David's business acumen and considerable intellect (with Masters degrees in Theology and Economics) are put to great use for charities and the national Anabaptist Steering Group.

**Jo,** a West-Midlands social worker, eco-activist, peace campaigner. Professionally Jo has moved between local authority social work and time with eco-charities; now she also leads a newly forming Peace Church.

**Jon,** a North-Wales former teacher, community activist, allotmenteer. Jon lives quietly (living off the rental income from his parental home) but three or four times per year, he gathers a handful of folks for a week's teaching, discussion, and visits, imbuing them with a vision for "a radical alternative life", which he continues to mentor. His partner, Morag, is a local authority education adviser.

**Jonathan,** a Yorkshire committed self (house) builder, medical consultant, local Anabaptist group co-ordinator.

Jonathan is a passionate advocate of Anabaptism, whose nurturing of local interest is leading to the formation of an Anabaptist congregation

**Mark,** a Lincolnshire organic smallholder, herb-grower, jazz musician, Quaker. Mark lives with his wife, two lodgers, three cats, two goats, umpteen chickens and keeps bees in four locations. They downshifted from city life and now deliver their organic veg, honey and world wholefoods to local shops.

**Sue**, a Fens primary school teacher, passionate cyclist, permaculturist. Sue, "now happily divorced", lives with her aging aunt as a companion; together they make wine and knit bespoke cardigans to order. Sue also plays keyboard in both a local pub band and the nearby Methodist chapel.

**Trisha,** an Oxford freelance proof-reader and book editor, church secretary, fabric crafts maker. Trisha downsized her life to enrich its quality; she co-hosted her local group, loves knitting and quilt-making and has just helped to oversee a church site redeveloped as flats for the homeless.

# Further Reading

I hope you want to learn some more about Anabaptism. Those who wish to follow particular themes or academic strands should find that following the foot-noted book references will lead to the next level of resources. In the interim, I hope that you may find these suggestions helpful.

*Anabaptist History and Theology,* C. Arnold Snyder, Ontario: Pandora Press, 1995.

As it says on the tin: this is the standard academic text delineating the history and theology, providing avenues for fuller study; a less expensive students' edition is also available.

*Artists, Citizens, Philosophers*, Duane K. Friesen, Scottdale: Herald Press, 2000.

A stimulating read, which attempts to offer an Anabaptist theology of culture. It makes a vital claim for Anabaptists to be involved in developing the civic life at every level in different spheres.

*Body Politics*, John Howard Yoder, Nashville: Discipleship Resources, 1992.

A slim volume (88pp) exploring five distinctive practices of Anabaptist 'communities of believers' showing why they have importance for the breadth of radical Christian witness.

*Journey Towards Holiness*, Alan Kreider, Basingstoke: Marshalls, 1986.

Exactly what it says – a personal and biblical exploration of the holiness vocation to discipleship from a clear (but little said) Anabaptist perspective.

*The Believer's Church*, Donald Durnbaugh, Scottdale: Herald Press, 1968.

An easily readable volume detailing the history and character of radical Protestantism, covering many different movements A to Z: think Anabaptists to Zinzendoirf's Moravian connection.

*The Naked Anabaptist,* Stuart Murray, Carlisle: Paternoster, 2010.

A well-written, but warts-and-all, defence of the Anabaptist cause, covering similar ground to this volume but with extra analysis of both strengths and weaknesses.

*The Politics of Jesus,* John Howard Yoder, Grand Rapids: Eerdmans, 1994.

For many, Yoder's seminal work demonstrating Jesus as political Messiah, challenging the complicity of state and religious authority in their unjust control of people's lives.

*The Upside-down Kingdom,* Donald B. Kraybill, Scottdale: Herald Press, 1990.

A joyfully challenging book to nurture Anabaptist discipleship; it makes a great study book for a weekly home-group or weekend house-party.

*When War is Unjust,* John Howard Yoder, Maryknoll: Orbis, 1996.

This offers a critical framework to re-evaluate the western 'just-war' tradition, building arguments towards a credible alternative for peace-makers and academics alike.

*Why Not Celebrate?* Sara Wenger Shenk, Intercourse: Good Books, 1990.

A delightful compendium of ideas, worship resources and food suggestions, for extended families, house-parties and 'communities of believers' sharing the liturgical year and personal milestones.

# Acknowledgements

I am grateful to many friends and mentors – Anabaptists, Menonites, Quakers and others – whose questioning and encouragement led to the writing of this book. Particular mention is needed of those in the Anabaptist Network's Steering Group and from the London Mennonite Centre, both trustees and staff, whose reading of parts of this book or conversation helped forge its shape and content.

Formal thanks needs to be noted to Priscilla Trenchard, the artist of the 'Cross-Dove', used by permission from LMC's trustees for the cover of this book. My particular gratitude is due to Allan Armstrong, Sarah Lane Cawte, Trisha Dale, Stuart Murray and Jeremy Thomson, whose specific help and incisive comments sharpened the narrative's focus.

Again, I am grateful to both Jeremy for his gracious foreword and to Allan and his team at Antioch Books for their editorial help and support. In the end the responsibility for the text and its direction is mine, as is the responsibility for any historical inaccuracies and other errors.

To those who have been so supportive – Sarah and Mark, Paul and Chris, Philip and Kathryn, Janice, Keith and Annie, Roger P, the *Growzone* team, the 'Windsor Crowd' and Princeton friends – who have provided meals, CDs, lots of good questions and quiet corners to read and write: thank you all. And finally to you, the reader, thanks for buying this book – may God bless your reading and response.

Andrew Francis
Ascension Tide, 2010